10 Steps to Cultural Proficiency

by Casaundra Monique McNair, Ed.D.

10 Steps to Cultural Proficiency by Casaundra Monique McNair
Copyright © 2017 by Casaundra Monique McNair; McNair Publishing

All rights reserved. No part of this book may be reproduced or transmitted in any form or by any means, electronic or mechanical, including photocopying, recording, or by any information storage and retrieval system without written permission of the author.

Library of Congress Cataloging-in-Publication Data
By: Casaundra Monique McNair
    10 Steps to cultural proficiency

ISBN 978-0-9993973-05

P.O. Box 2610
Moreno Valley, CA 92554
www.casaundramcnair.com

Cover Design: Clinton Hopkins "CLON"

Dedication

This book is dedicated to all those who want to make a difference in schools, businesses, churches and other organizations. There are many schools of thought of what defines an educator, but you all are! Also, there are many theories regarding ways to obtain cultural proficiency using a cultural proficiency continuum (Lindsey, Robins & Terrell, 2003) and the like, but this book does not use the continuum. This book takes on a different approach that goes through 10 different steps that can impact the culture in which you live starting today!

TABLE OF CONTENTS

PREFACE vii

STEP ONE 1

STEP TWO 10

STEP THREE 15

STEP FOUR 21

STEP FIVE 29

STEP SIX 42

STEP SEVEN 48

STEP EIGHT 56

STEP NINE 62

STEP TEN 66

REFERENCES 69

Preface

I know what you're thinking.... this is just ANOTHER book about culture and equity in schools; well, not really! In an era where schools are becoming more segregated by programs, socioeconomic status, social and cultural capital, we must think about the inequities that exist. We must consider the frame of reference of the stakeholders for our local schools; our state senators and assemblymen, our district employees, our city government, our local schools, our colleagues, our families, but most of all, our students that we have signed up to serve. As society changes, we must realize that sometimes our students are coming into schools different from what we have remembered; but we all have the same goal of educating all the students sitting in front of us. Additionally, if we are in a role that plays a part in the production of productive members in society, we are ALL educators. Someone is watching how we walk, talk, and follow through with our purpose; therefore we are all educators.

The Historical Perspective of Social Justice Education

In examining the concepts of educating students and being culturally relevant, we cannot negate social justice and the concepts of equity. In that, one must identify and understand the issues that exist between the dominant culture and those not apart of the dominant culture. In the United States, most of the time, the culture or racial/ethnic group that is seen as the dominant culture is White culture. However, in certain situations it is not. The dominant culture has been defined as the group of people who may even be a minority in number, but one that holds the power, the wealth and the decision making control for other groups of individuals (Irvine & Armento, 2001). With regard to equity, we have all seen the 3 students at the fence attempting to look through it. What we find is that equality is providing the students with the same thing and expecting them to succeed, where equity is giving them what they need in order to succeed. Therefore in this text, equity is providing students with educators around them that are culturally proficient. With the development and internalization of culturally relevant strategies, students and educators alike will begin seeing more inclusive education and higher academic achievement rates.

There are a variety of angles you can examine in social justice, from funds of knowledge (Moll, Amanti, Neff, Gonzalez, 1992), to critical theory that exposes schools who "generates and reproduces inequities" (Foster, 1986, p. 20), to whiteness as property, and one who uses a multidimensional ethical framework (Starratt, 1994). This framework combines to form a "human and ethical response to unethical and challenging environments and situations for marginalized groups" (p. 20). Marginalized groups defined as groups who may seem like the "others" and what some researchers consider, "othered" (Kumashiro, 2000). With the "other" being represented by those who are other than the norm, a person of color, underemployed, unemployed, female, or of the LGBT (Lesbian, Gay, Bisexual, Transgender) or queer community. In todays schools the concept of being the "other" is also referred to in terms as "those kids" or a kid who may not belong because they come from "the other side of the tracks" or a low socioeconomic neighborhood.

In order to be an educator and a leader for social justice and equity, one must also have strong ethics and a list of non-negotiables in order to change the root of the problem, which we will discuss in a later step. As Ciulla

(2004) defines it, "leadership is not a person or a position. It is a complex moral relationship between people, based on trust, obligation, commitment, emotion, and a shared vision of the good" (p. xv). "Ethics is about how we distinguish between right and wrong, or good and evil in relation to the actions, volitions, and character of human beings" (p. xv). This should be at the base of how all decisions are made by leaders for their constituents in the society in which we live. An educator without ethics is truly criminal.

If we are all working towards the goal of students experiencing a socially just education; as Blackmore (2002) purports, "educational leaders must practice moral outrage", they must "defend and extend principles of human dignity" and they must "restructure the market models to improve social relations and conditions of learning" (p. 23). I purport that they must do that and more. They must seek to change the paradigm and the master narrative that has been spoken over our students and the educational system by the dominant culture.

Educational Paradigms

Social justice leadership is something great leaders arrive it. It is not a usual starting point. Most educational leaders in America are used to operating educational institutions the same way the world is ran, via social class systems. Howard (2010) states, "cultural responsive pedagogy embodies a professional, political, cultural, ethical, and ideological disposition that supersedes mundane teaching acts; it is centered in fundamental beliefs about teaching, learning, students, their families, and their communities, and an unyielding commitment to see student success become less rhetoric and more of a reality" (p.

67).

Through this pedagogy, teachers and administrators are challenged to commit to teaching in a way that responds to the different cultures that walk into today's schools. It is another way schools must respond to the "ongoing achievement disparities between African American and Latino students, and their White and certain Asian American counterparts" (pg. 68). If we do not begin to walk in socially just practices, more and more students will be left behind. Irvine and Armento (2001) state, "culturally responsive teaching is not a novel or transformative approach to teaching…" They continue by stating it has been around U.S. schools for "centuries, but it has been most responsive to one group of students- U.S. born middle class, English-speaking, White students" (pg. 71), the dominant culture. However, this approach often requires a charismatic authoritative approach to leadership in order to execute appropriately (Bouie, 2012, p. 8). Without someone that is leading as a warm demander, progress will come to a standstill.

Nevertheless, it is important to identify that schools are beginning to sincerely challenge the educators within the walls of the schoolhouse to systematically respond to the "chronic academic underachievement of culturally diverse and low-income students" (Howard, 2010, pg. 69). One thing I see challenging for my fellow educators who have been in the classrooms for a long period of time is the mindset of how to approach curriculum design and lessons which will encourage the student's creativity and learning without inducing trauma and other forms of discrimination which results in students of color performing lower than their white counterparts. Howard (2010) asserts that teachers must be familiar with a variety of teaching pedagogy in order to tap into what students know, to ultimately engage them in the learning process (p. 76). This is vital if today's schools are going to achieve success. Nevertheless, it is challenging because it questions the belief systems of some educators.

The other angle of challenging the existing paradigm in education is the concept that "all teachers are political, whether they are conscious to it or not" (Shannon, 2001, p. 2). With the political consciousness teachers knowingly and unknowingly posses, schooling is either dominating or liberating to students based off of the philosophy of the instructor. The dominating schooling includes the "indoctrination, acculturation, and standardization" of education which has a static worldview and Freire's (1970) concept of the banking model. This model has a purpose of reproducing the status quo student. This teaching model is catering to the essentialism and perennialism point of view. Both of these views stem from a Eurocentric perspective with many rote memory skills tested which include a lack of text depth and complexity (Mirci, 2007). Young (1990) describes the five faces of oppression and it is under dominating school culture where students who are not apart of the dominant culture are exploited, marginalized, powerless, experience cultural imperialism and violence.

The liberating view of education challenges the existing paradigm because it has an evolutionary point of view. It is a model catering to pragmatism and progressivism philosophy. Its aim is to change society through the lens of social change agentry and social reconstructivism to create a society, which is socially just. Under this paradigm shift is where multiculturalism (Banks, 2006) in curriculum is exposed. It is the place where critically relevant pedagogy and socially just curriculum is used and is free to be expressed (Howard, 2010). As Minow, Shweder & Marksus (2008) explain, students under a liberalistic perspective have the autonomy to be who they are. They are seen as equals. There is the opportunity for merit-based justice (virtue), equal opportunity (welfare) and care (benevolent safe-keeping). It is considered as an equal opportunity to anyone who desires it. Sandel (2009) discusses how it is a human freedom for individuals to live their life in the way they choose. But do we do this as educators? Or do we continue to as our predecessors have often done and totally place our ideologies on the students and classrooms that we are in? At the end of the day, it should students should have more of the freedom of choice. In libertarianism it is all about fairness and freedom. It is important to note libertarianism "holds that justice requires respect for whatever choices people make, provided the choices don't violate anyone's rights" (Sandel, 2009, p. 96). Putting it together, there is a way to provide students with choice with order. They can coexist.

Furthermore, Immanuel Kant states that morality should be "exercised... through pure practical reason." He continues to argue, "every person is worthy of respect, not because we ourselves but because we are rational beings, capable of reason; we are also autonomous beings, capable of acting and choosing freely" (Sandel, 2009, p. 107). With the a variety choices of freedom, many theories were birthed from this instructional methodology, Critical Theory (Horkheimer & Adorno, 1972), Critical Race Theory (Delgado & Stefancic, 2001), Feminist Theory (Rich, 1996), Queer Theory (Berlant & Freeman, 1992) and Post-Colonial Theory (Chia, 2008).

With varying degrees of freedom that exist, we also must introduce the concept of instant gratification. Many of our students and even their families are so used to instant gratification. The teaching doesn't seem fast enough, comments like "school is boring" "I don't like my teacher," "I wish my teacher knew…" echo through our school hallways and playgrounds. Our society has become racially charged with slurs aimed to demean someone's character. Unfortunately, it has become a part of the norm. Even the name calling by many high ranking officials in our government have sent the signs and signals to our colleagues, parents and students that it is an okay practice to have. With all the issues that surround race and culture in schools, are you OR your stakeholders equipped to discuss the social issues that exist? Black Lives Matter, Blue Lives Matter, All Lives Matter?

Now that we have set a base for education and reviewing educational paradigms; you may ask yourself, why do I need to be culturally proficient? Can't someone else do it? No, no one else can do it. It is YOUR story, your belief and your experience that add to improving the teaching and learning for all students. By being culturally proficient, you will realize that culture is central to all learning because it shapes the thinking process of individuals. Lastly, through your learning, this book is designed to cause you to reflect on your current and future practices of serving diverse students and their families. The first five steps are highly theoretical with the base of critical pedagogy, but brief and reflective. Whereas the last five steps are designed to be slightly theoretical, but practical, again causing you to reflect and then ignite you to be a change agent within and beyond your sphere of influence. If you are ready…. Let's go!

STEP 1
~Understanding Culture~

"Preservation of one's own culture does not require contempt or disrespect for other cultures." ~ Cesar Chavez

When thinking about culture, you must consider more than just race and ethnicity. Race and ethnicity are very important; but do you understand the community you are serving in? Can you answer the following questions: Do you know the average median income of your school? Do you know the median age of your community? Do you know the average median household value? Do you know the top 3 employers of the city? Do you know the crime rate? Within your school, do you know what stores and business are located within your school attendance boundary? Do you know the ethnic demographics of not only your school, but the community? Thinking inside of your school; have you examined your discipline data? Have you discussed it with other colleagues? Have you examined to see if disproportionality has been considered to see if you are even cognizant of your own trends? Have equity and equality just become a buzzword for the educators in your building? Does asset-based or deficit-based thinking exist in your building?

You're probably asking, why all the questions? Why is this important? This is important because you need to be able to assess how you will serve your community. Being an educator in a culturally diverse community means more than just knowing the race of the students you serve and knowing a little bit of their slang. Don't get me wrong, that is good, you need that; but knowing how to relate to the needs of the students will assist you even more.

Looking beyond the levels of questioning described above, Hammond (2015) talks about three types of culture. Surface, shallow and deep culture. In schools we deal in surface and shallow culture. Surface is observable, it carries a low emotional charge; it is the type of culture that we are usually okay with exchanging with people we don't know. We have become okay with sharing and discussing music genres, food choices, and sometimes holidays we celebrate. It carries a low emotional charge because it is something we can usually see with the naked eye.

Shallow culture is more like the unspoken rules that surround everyday social interactions that include mostly non-verbal communication like personal space, why someone would look you in the eye to have a conversation and why he or she would not. Shallow culture is something educators as a whole have become better at. Especially in the cases of schools with high immigrant populations; shallow culture is more examined and respected by the different languages being spoken in homes across America. Deep culture is where our extensive feelings and unconscious assumptions govern how we see the world. It carries an intense emotional charge because it is the part of an individual's culture where their spirituality, health, and ethics lie. This type of culture has historically been said as things not to talk about in the workplace because of the emotional charge that it can carry. However, when deep culture is never discussed, it leaves room for the emotional charge to grow due to the misunderstandings that can occur. This is usually due to misunderstandings between people.

Now, assessing the types of culture that is prevalent in your school building or in your environment is a necessary first step to cultural proficiency. You will not become culturally proficient until you realize the levels of culture that exist in your immediate environment. It is equally important for you to note the level in which you operate. If you hold a supervisory role, examining culture also means how much are you willing to give of yourself? How much conflict are you potentially ready to mediate, as in some cases this will be the first time that one has ever examined things further than just surface culture.

Equity Audit

Another angle that has been used to address cultural irrelevance is equity audits. In schools they can be tools to guide personnel in working toward equity and excellence via the use of auditing in civil rights, curriculum auditing, and state accountability policy systems (Skrla, et al., 2009; Skrla, et al, 2010). Equity audits focus on providing qualitative measures of accountability that will adequately address, and subsequently correct, the achievement gap existing between African Americans, other underrepresented minorities, and white students who represent the dominant culture and student population in the United States. The historical background of equity audits stems from the Civil Rights Act of 1964, which "prohibits race, color, and national origin discrimination" (p. 263). However, since 1964, there has been little progress in eradicating discriminating practices in education, they still exist. Skrla et al. (2010) asserts, "equity audits, which has roots in U.S. educational and civil rights history, that we have redesigned, simplified and streamlined to be of maximum utility in the current climate of high-stakes accountability, and readily available data" (p. 262) has been poorly used.

Within equity audits, Riehl (2000) explores the notion of building relationships in such a high accountability environment with diverse students in areas where diversity hasn't been a factor may cause some critical issues. Issues that causes the instructional leader to not only be a deliberate change agent, but one who operates subjectively to look at operating in more of an inclusive way; thus implementing more inclusive practices in schools. As Drake & Goldring (2014) emphasize, "these partnerships include transformative, inclusive, and social justice model of leadership which proactively seeks equity and cultural responsiveness and reach out to marginalized students and families" (p. 48). With this reflection of practice, one should be reaching out to marginalized students and families ultimately helping to close the achievement gap. However, the achievement gap will continue to widen when there is no one advocating for such groups. Therefore one has to be the change and understand the culture around you.

Equity audits assist with providing the information to examine what is happening and see if and when a particular racial or ethnic group is being marginalized. In response to the call to action by the Department of Education, many states have developed updated accountability systems to highlight their champion of equity or the inequities that exist. For example, if you are in California, you can review your California Dashboard to get more information about where you are as a county, school district and as a school. If not, seek out your State Department of Education to see how your schools are measuring.

Race in the United States

Race is an issue that has plagued our nation for decades. It is prevalent in communities, schools, and in our classrooms. Concepts of race link to critical race theory, due to their connection with how deeply it affects the society in which we live. As Closson's (2010) study on critical race theory and adult education argued, "Our society is structured with systemic racism. When we accept racism as endemic, we accept that everyone is infected with a disease to greater or lesser degrees. Whites suffer from White privilege; Blacks suffer from internalized racism" (p. 279).

This point accentuates the extent to which race is a factor everywhere and everyone is affected by it. DuBois(1961) declared, "The problem of the twentieth century is the problem of the color-line" (p. 23). Many authors echoed this sentiment by asserting race is a social construct; it is not biological. It derives from what has been made of it in society (Brown & Jackson, 2013; Chang, 2002; DuBois, 1961; Hayman & Levit, 2002; Hill, 2008; Howard, 2010; Matsuda, Lawrence, Delgado, & Crenshaw, 1993; O'Connor, Hill, & Robinson, 2009; Rabaka, 2013; West, 1993; Zamundio et al., 2011).

Howard (2010) explained race is a "self-prescribed and externally ascribed meaning" (p. 96), which furthers the belief that some people do not recognize why they believe what they believe; it becomes an unconscious bias. In fact, race is more social and political than something with an actual biological meaning (Brown & Jackson, 2013; Chang, 2002; DuBois, 1961; Hayman & Levit, 2002; Hill, 2008; Howard, 2010; Matsuda et al., 1993; O'Conner et al., 2009; Rabaka, 2013; West, 1993; Zamundio et al., 2011). Because this is true, the United States as a whole views race more than what scientists have believed race is. Everywhere you turn, someone is referring to another person by the color of his or her skin. Because of this, children begin forming the habit of referring to someone by race or ethnicity. Additionally, one cannot assess what they believe without the "analysis of race in schools . . . [and] what meanings educators assign to students who come from racially diverse groups" (Howard, 2010, p. 96).

As Gillborn (2005), asserted, "educational policy is an act of White supremacy" (p. 502). This statement holds true because our current history books are written from a Eurocentric perspective. Because of this, White culture is usually being portrayed and sometimes taught as superior.

Race has been used as a social rating tool for a long time (Zamundio et al., 2011). Many people use race as a tool for their belief system and, based on the racial group they belong, they determine what students should be able to do. They further emphasized if someone says that race doesn't matter in the 21st Century, they are not being honest. Zamundio et al. (2011) stated, "The very notion that race no longer matters is part of an ideology that justifies and legitimates racial inequality in society" (p. 3). This type of thinking continues to perpetuate the notion that the racial inequality conversation has no place in our schools.

In Howard's (2010) discussion on race theory and its implications for education, he connects how as explanations become clearer concerning what race and racism have to do with the widespread failure of students of color, then we are able to understand the wide influences of inequality, discrimination, and, most important, race and racism, and how they may influence achievement disparities (p. 99). Gillborn (2006) discussed that many schools are not doing much to address the racial inequities that exist. He said it seems that most are "complacent about their duties and uninterested in further progress" (p. 6). As Dr. Cornel West (1993) stated, "Blackness has no meaning outside of a system of race-conscious people and practices" (p. 25). Thus, changes need to be made. Sometimes it seems as if many want to just say they are colorblind and as one of my students in a university class once said, "can we just leave race at the door of the classroom and just teach?" This type of mindset halts any progress that has been made. If students were asked to leave their race and culture at the door, what would our classrooms look like? What would we produce?

Howard (2010) spoke about the four different approaches in the continuum of race. The first one is that race is nonessential approach contends that race and/or racism has nothing to do with the current academic outcomes of students in U.S. schools, and refutes any inquiry that even raises the racial question or seeks analysis along racial lines (McWhorter, 2000; S. Steele, 1990; Thernstrom & Thernstrom, 2003)" (p. 92). Others have argued that minorities have failed in the United States because they were just too lazy to do what it takes to make it in society and not because of any particular institution and policy (Howard, 2010). Second on the race continuum is the "more liberal approach, race [is] essential" (Howard, 2010, p. 93). This comes from the notion of the United States being so deeply rooted in racism that it does not stand a chance to come out of those practices.

Third, on the continuum, Howard (2010) discussed, "race is the determining variable in all that ails schools and society approach" (p. 93). This point posits that racism is the common denominator for the differences in academia. It also contends that the history of racism is what has been the breeding ground for the "long history of . . . and racial exclusion[ary]" (Howard, 2010, p. 93) practices in education. Lastly on the continuum, a more balanced perspective and centers on the institutional responsibility–individual accountability approach. This approach assumes that race and racism have always played a significant role in the way life is experienced in the United States . . .

(Noguera, 2003; Tough, 2008). Most would say that this is where we currently are.

Now there has been progress, but "race remains relevant" (Howard, 2010, p. 93) it is something that is not disappearing any time soon. Howard postulated if change is to happen in educational institutions they would have to examine all parts including the hiring of personnel, classroom environments, and other areas surrounding student engagement in order to uncover racist practices. Furthermore, the notion of whiteness as property committed against students and their families, creates disproportionality in discipline, course access, and especially, special education, which perpetuates Howard's assertions.

Researchers agreed that achieving race equity requires a consistent fight for lawmakers as well as stakeholders in schools (Gillborn, 2013; Howard, 2010). Thus, with there being issues in discipline, course access, medical care and special education (e.g. under-representation, misdiagnosis from doctors, and under-serving of students), employing critical race theory as a lens to examine and gain a deeper understanding of the role of the parents and other educators like you is crucial.

Reflection

What does the culture of my school, district, or county look like? What does it feel like? How do I respond to difference? How do the educators around you respond to difference? What story does my data tell me?

STEP 2
~Understanding Point of View~

"If there is one secret of success, it lies in the ability to get the other person's point of view and see things from that person's angle as well as from your own"
~Henry Ford~

Your mindset can keep you lost in your own headspace. As Dweck (2006) writes in Mindsets, a fixed mindset is what keeps one stagnant. Having a fixed mindset can cause one to think they have no need to continue to learn and to continue to evolve because their mind is set on where they are and that being all they need to be successful in life. A fixed mindset has no place in the quest to becoming culturally proficient. When a person with a fixed mindset encounters a culture different from theirs or someone operating at a different level of culture than they are; they treat that person the way they have seen the treatment of that person portrayed in their family, in social situations and in the media. It is the way that has been engrained in their mind at birth and it is set. It is often thought that ones view of someone else has everything to do with their socialization.

In a Long Walk to Freedom, Nelson Mandela states, "No one is born hating another person because of the color of his skin, or his background, or his religion. People must learn to hate, and if they can learn to hate, they can be taught to love, for love comes more naturally to the human heart than its opposite." Mandela implores us to recapitulate the time and place in which we live. In looking at the news, reading the newspaper, one could perceive that the all the hate in the world can be turned around if people began loving each other and teaching children how to love. This requires a growth mindset.

A growth mindset is one that promotes a mind of growth, independence and maturity. It is a mindset that is accepting of others and different points of view. A growth mindset sees cultural relevance as an opportunity, not a hindrance to educational growth. An individual with a growth mindset looks for ways to improve current practice;

one is also a reflective thinker who focuses on ways to continue to be persistent in the face of adversity. But one must know what their non-negotiables are so they don't sway when adversity comes.

Non-Negotiables

A negotiable is something that is open for discussion or something that is open to modifications. When thinking about your point of view, one subconsciously negotiates his or her response to a situation. However, when one is negotiating it leaves room for your perspective to be changed by someone or something. On the contrary, a non-negotiable is when a thought, belief or feeling is not open for discussion and/or modification. Non-negotiables are often times called beliefs or values for different people. For example, if you believed that one should not murder another person, but then someone injures or kills one of your family members; you could change that belief based off of this new circumstance. However, a non-negotiable would mean that despite what may happen to me, I would still believe that murder is wrong and would not want to murder anyone.

I often discuss non-negotiables when I teach pre-service teachers. I encourage them to think about their non-negotiables in the classroom, what would they tolerate, what would not they tolerate. I challenge them to consider the measures are they willing to take to ensure a student succeeds? What things are they willing to do to ensure all their students receive equitable education? I think it is important for non-classroom practitioners to consider what their non-negotiables are before they enter into practice to prevent any unknown issues or any compromising circumstances. This is something that in your practice is not up for discussion. One may say, I will not tolerate any mistreatment of any student. Due to this non-negotiable, that person could be seen as an advocate. This would mean, they would speak up if and when they see a student being mishandled by an adult. Although this may mean that if they speak up, they put themselves in a position to be looked at differently than the next person due to past practice. But on the road to cultural proficiency, it is likely one may need to have ongoing conversations with educators who seem as if they do not know how to navigate working with a students that are different. This is good because it creates a space for educators and adults that work with our students to come to realize that they must be the change if one expects our students to know their worth and also begin to treat each other differently.

Reflection

Have you ever spent time to think about what your non-negotiables are? This is applicable to parents, teacher, administrators, central office staff and anyone who works with students. I want you to spend some time reflecting in your sphere of influence, what are your non-negotiables?

As a parent, in reviewing the needs of my child; the following are non-negotiables:
_____
_____
_____
_____
_____
_____

As a teacher, the following are non-negotiables in my classroom:

_____
_____
_____
_____
_____

As an administrator, the following are the non-negotiables at my site:

_____
_____
_____
_____
_____

As a central office staff member, the following are the non-negotiables:

_____
_____
_____
_____
_____

As a _____, the following are my non-negotiables:

STEP 3 ~Understanding Capital & Privilege~

"I would like to make it so that education was a right, and not a privilege." ~Daphne Koeller~

Before getting into privilege let's discuss capital. As discussed in step one, many authors echo the sentiment that asserts race is a social construct; it is not biological. It derives from what has been made of it in society (Brown & Jackson, 2013; Chang, 2002; DuBois, 1961; Hayman & Levit, 2002; Hill, 2008; Howard, 2010; Matsuda, Lawrence, Delgado, & Crenshaw, 1993; O'Connor, Hill, & Robinson, 2009; Rabaka, 2013; West, 1993; Zamundio et al., 2011). This results in society creating a class system based off of race. So I ask again, what does race mean to you?

If that is not a question one can outright answer without hesitation I would suggest you began examining your unconscious bias. Unconscious bias meaning the way you think and the biases you have toward certain people and certain groups. Consider, what was your journey in school like? Who treated you differently because of the color of your skin? Who treated you differently based off of the jobs your parents held? Who have you treated differently because of the color of their skin or socioeconomic status? Who was treated differently by the teachers who taught you? Was it a racial issue?

Social Capital.

Sociologist James Coleman and French social theorist Pierre Bourdieu are recognized for being the front-runners of introducing social capital in the context of school and culture (Portes, 2000). Social capital can be viewed in three different ways. It can be seen as a source of social control, a source of family meditated benefits, and a source of resources meditated by nonfamily networks (Portes, 1998; Coleman, 1988). Coleman (1988) discusses the different forms of social capital and how one is able to obtain it. Social capital can be defined by who you know, your environment, and the education of those around you. Bourdieu defines social capital "as something requires both cultural and economic resources" (Bourdieu, 1989). It is something that can be created but it requires connections with other people to make it happen. Portes (1998) defines economic capital as something someone has it in their bank, human capital is all in the mind, and social capital is all in who you are related to and who you know. Freire (1970) also refers to this, as the banking model where all someone knows is what has been provided to him or her by someone else. In many of our schools social capital is prevalent in the way students are accessing courses, receiving scholarships and other preferential treatment.

Human Capital.

Klebanov & Brooks-Gunn (2006) explain human capital to include "parental education, employment, and welfare receipt" (p. 64). In their study on human capital and intelligence quotient (IQ), they discovered that human capital risks are highly correlated to children and their declines in their IQ. It is said "more educated parents talk more to their children, use less harsh discipline techniques, spend more time teaching their children, and provide more stimulating environments, all of which contribute to higher cognitive scores (p. 75). Thus, the more educated a parent is, the more they instill in their children and the better educated they will be. Now this is just research, but there are many families with much resiliency that instill the same value in their children with or without money. They desire for their children to be greater than them so they use the human capital investment strategy to get their children ahead.

Human capital investment strategy is important to economist because it is understood; it is what a person has within themselves (Galor & Tsiddon, 1997; Benabou, 1996; Wayne, Linden, Kraimer, Graf, 1999). Additionally, it has been proven learning begins much earlier than when a student attends a classroom for the very first time (Heckman & Masterov, 2004; Heckman, et al., 2006). Students pick up the behaviors from what is taught in the home. If students have a highly structured environment, they usually embrace the classroom setting. If the students have a free flowing environment with no structure, they do not embrace the order of the classroom setting. Heckman (1999) explains, "the role of the family is crucial to the formation of learning skills, and government interventions at an early age that mend the harm done by dysfunctional families have proven to be highly effective (p. 50). Therefore, it has been concluded more money should be placed in early intervention to assist with the low human capital students are beginning school with (Heckman et al., 2006; McLoyd, 1998). With this, families that can send their students to preschool is valuable to the foundational success of a student.

On the other side, due to highly dysfunctional families that exist in society, many children are coming to school ill-equipped to handle the challenges before them. Therefore it is important for educators to understand the "out of school factors" that exist. Berliner (2006) asserts educators need to consider the out of school factors before they start blaming themselves for not doing something and make changes to a system that may be flawed, but not broken. He argues that in a course of a school year, students may spend around 1000 hours in school and about five times that with their families and in their neighborhoods during the year. With these statistics, it can be argued that the human capital that is being built during this time is either positive or negative, but it is definitely up to the parents and the situations they allow their child to enter into, which determines the effect it will have.

Cultural Capital.
Bourdieu (1986) theory of cultural capital discusses how it is not something that could be understood in isolation, but is a concept with relation to the social and human capital a family may have. It comes in 3 forms, the embodied state (long lasting in the mind and body), the objectified state (cultural goods that take material form) and the institutionalized state (the economics of the cultural goods in society). Most educational justice leaders apply social and cultural capital together with the consideration of human capital. In theory, it is difficult to apply one without the other. Culture is central to learning, so without culture, students are just shells.

Privilege
Now that you understand culture, race and the concept of equity, privilege has been defined as "a special right, advantage, or immunity granted or available only to a particular person or group of people" (Merriam-Webster, 2017). When there is unconscious bias, some form of privilege is usually present. American sociologist, Michael Kimmel (2009), describes privilege as something that people have and usually don't notice. For example, one may say, you run like you are running with the wind at your back. Well many are unaware the reason they are able

to run faster is because of the force of the wind. Likewise to privilege, one doesn't realize they are able to get ahead because there is something present that has existed long before them.

When I think about privilege, I think about the sense of entitlement some arrive at. It is sometimes viewed as the rejection of a program that would benefit the dominant culture instead of one that increases equity. For example, white privilege has often been portrayed to be when one is a part of the dominant culture and they are granted certain rights and privileges just because of who they are or who they know. As Closson (2010) asserted, "Whites suffer from White privilege [and] Blacks suffer from internalized racism" (p. 279). Thus, in order to overcome the isolation and ridicule or to avoid it, many parents and homes empower themselves with self-education and formal education in order to advocate effectively. Let's get educated!

Reflection

What culture do I most identify with? Have I recognized my own privilege? How does my privilege affect others?

STEP 4 ~Understanding the Diverse Learner~

"We are more alike than different, but we are all individuals, with unique abilities and needs." ~ Author Unknown

In today's schools, educators are experiencing more and more diverse learners. In many classrooms and schools, there are learners who have become the exception to the typically developing student. While there still remain students who would be considered our typically developing students; in many of our schools they are becoming the minority. A typically developing student is one identified as one that turns in their homework on time, has no behavior infractions, completes test and quizzes with proficiency, attends school regularly, has a stable home structure that provides support for them after they leave school grounds.

However, more and more are educators discovering that we have families with an atypical set up. There are families with not only single parent households, but families with two parents that have to work more than one job each just to provide for the family; thus leaving the children home with no parents and no assistance to complete out of school tasks. There are family structures with grandparents, guardians, neighbors and even televisions raising children. Yes, I said televisions. Many parents are allowing their children to sit in front of the television all day during their early developmental years, sometimes not realizing it is setting the stage for a dysfunctional student. This contributes to the notion that since televisions are raising children, they are losing the social connection and familial connection because their parents are disconnected. This disconnection contributes to the lack of soft skills in students that were at one time developed in the home environment.

I think about a student I had named John (pseudo name). John was a five-year-old Kindergartner who would yell and scream every day when he started the school year.

Upon closer examination, his teacher and I discovered that John had never been asked to sit in a chair. Even when discussing the weekend events with the parents, the parent indicated they never took John to church or to a restaurant because he would not sit still. So unfortunately because his parent never taught him that skill early on, his teacher and I were then tasked to teach him the skill as well as partner with the family to ensure it continued once he went home after five years of never been asked to. John is recognized as a diverse learner. Although he came to school with some academic skills, he came from a background where structure was not the norm. Therefore, once in a structured environment he rejected it and did not know how to respond. If his teacher had not accepted the fact his upbringing was different from the one she experienced, they would have stopped there and not have been able to look past the out of school factors and concern themselves with only what they could control in making better outcomes for John.

Special Education

Another type of diverse learner is a special education student. Special education has a long history in education. Beginning at the cusp of the civil rights era, Brown v. Board of Education (1954) was a landmark decision marking the beginning of new conversations regarding educational segregation. The ruling of Brown v. Board of Education demanded the desegregation of schools and created a "15-year period of unprecedented legal, political, economic, and educational measures directed towards dismantling the structures of racism and oppression instituted as a result of segregation" (Brown & Jackson, 2013, p. 9). However, no one did anything after the ruling to immediately desegregate the schools

(McGuinn, 2006). The Brown v. Board of Education (1955) stated schools must integrate "with all deliberate speed" (p. 27); but unfortunately it did not happen overnight.

Reviewing the Brown v. Board of Education (1955) decision, the notion of progressive action was a misnomer. The time span of the different phases of the case was over 12 years, which became very time consuming and not incredibly progressive. For example, during the stage of absolute defiance (1955 – 1959), most educational institutions did absolutely nothing. It seemed as if the more Blacks in a geographic area, the greater the fear, the more oppressive they would be (Wilkinson, 1978). During the second phase of token compliance (1959 – 1964), it ended with the Civil Rights Act of 1964, ending segregation in "any place of public accommodation" (Sec. 201. (a)). During the modest integration phase (1964 – 1968), which was at the beginning of the Civil Rights Act, courts knew it wasn't just about them anymore and they began seeing desegregation in other places besides schools. Finally, during the massive integration phase (1968), Judge Wisdom who presided over the Green v. County School Board of New Kent County explained school integration was not an option; it was an order. With all of this legislation happening beginning with the Civil Rights Era, cases regarding children with disabilities were next on the docket.

In 1972, a landmark case in Pennsylvania went to the courts, the Pennsylvania Association for Retarded Children (PARC) v. Commonwealth of Pennsylvania (1972). In this case, the State Board of Education (SBE) decided that they were not obligated to educate any child that was certified uneducable or un-trainable. Parents of children with disabilities residing in Pennsylvania then sought the support of the Department of Welfare. This agency did not agree they were under any obligation to educate the students. The case resulted in the Commonwealth of Pennsylvania denying a child's due process and equal protection under the United States Constitution by denying them an education. Soon after PARC v. Commonwealth of Pennsylvania (1972), there was Mills v. Board of Education of the District of Columbia in 1972, which was more of the same, a denial of education due to disability. Due to the cases above, the federal government had to do something (Alexander & Alexander, 2009).

In 1975, the Education of All Handicapped Children's Act (EAHCA, 1975), also known as Public Law 142 (PL-142) was established. This federal law required all students to receive a Free and Appropriate Public Education for Students with Disabilities (FAPE, 2010), that they must be educated in the Least Restrictive Environment (LRE), and that each student who qualifies for services in schools must have an Individualized Education Program (IEP). This program was designed to ensure all students access to the general education curriculum through program accommodations, modifications, and set academic goals.

To conform with Least Restrictive Environment as defined in IDEIA 2004, school districts must ensure to the maximum extent appropriate, that children with disabilities are educated with children who are not disabled (Alexander & Alexander, 2009; Kemerer & Sanson, 2009). Alexander and Alexander (2009), stated that

> Removal of children with disabilities from the regular education environment occurs only when

the nature of the severity of the disability of a child is such that education in regular classes with the use of supplementary aides and services cannot be achieved satisfactorily. (p. 592)

Therefore, with the combination of Education of All Handicapped Children's Act (EAHCA, 1975), Individuals with Disabilities Education Act (IDEA, 1975 cited in Center for Parent Information and Resources, 2014), and No Child Left Behind (NCLB, 2001), educators must use the Individualized Education Program (IEP) process to establish students with disabilities the Least Restrictive Environment (LRE) in schools.

Before EAHCA (1975), there were only two categories of special education students. The students were placed in classrooms according to their disabilities and treated either as educable or uneducable. Since EAHCA (1975), reauthorized as IDEIA (2004), students must have one or more of the 13 defined disabilities that requires instruction, services, or both, which cannot be provided with modification of the regular school program. The thirteen areas are,

(1) Autism [Autistic-like behaviors], (2) Deaf-blindness [hearing and visual impairments], (3) Deafness [hearing impairment], (4) Emotional disturbance [serious emotional disturbance], (5) Hearing impairment, (6) Mental Retardation, (7) Multiple Disabilities, (8) Orthopedic Impairment [severe orthopedic impairment], (9) Other Health Impairment [OHI], (10) Specific Learning Disability [SLD], (11) Speech and Language Impairment [SLI], (12) Traumatic Brain Injury [TBI], and (13) Visual Impairment. (Building the Legacy: IDEA, 2004, Sec. 300.8, (c))

In determining the Least Restrictive Environments for a student regardless of their disability, the students' IEP Team members must be present. There are both mandatory and discretionary members of that team. The mandatory members include one general education teacher, special education teacher, administrator, psychologist, (if assessment results are given), one parent, and, when appropriate, the student. The discretionary members can include educational advocates, attorneys, independent experts, evaluators, or anyone the parent or the team deems to be necessary for the child to receive educational benefit from the program. Together they decide the proper placement for the student. For a student to be improperly placed, it could be considered by law as a denial of her or his Free and Appropriate Public Education (Alexander & Alexander, 2009).

There are other diverse learners outside of students with special needs that exist. It is important for educators to think about the student that is twice exceptional. A twice-exceptional student is one who is identified for special education and Gifted and Talented Education (GATE) programs.

A GATE student is one that has "demonstrated or has potential abilities that give evidence of high performing capabilities." (CDE, 2005, p. 9). A GATE student usually participates in a program that offers academic differentiation that allows the student to show their intellectual, creative, talent in visual and performing arts or some other specialty. With ever changing laws and policies, it is important for you to seek out your local school district for their particular policy on gifted students and how one qualifies.

There is a legislative intent for GATE students

similar to special education students, as school districts are charged with having programs that will accommodate gifted students. Education Code Section 52200(c) and Assembly Bill (AB) 1040 enacted in 1998 establishes that each school district must create a program within the school day that caters to the gifted student. However, the law does not include direction on twice exceptional students. Thus it is important for educators to be mindful and create learning experiences that have enough differentiation to reach all students. Learning about the histories of the students and families in your school and community is vitally important in this aspect. This will assist you in becoming relevant as it pertains to culture difference in both gifted and special education student and their thoughts about differences in various ways in order to help you to develop a sensitivity to the community you serve.

Reflection

Do I recognize the diverse learners around me? How do I respond? Do I allow their limitations or their quirks keep me from having high expectations?

STEP 5
~Understand
Microaggressions~

"You are pretty for a black girl." ~anonymous~

"You are pretty for a black girl" is a phrase that many African American women experience at some time during their lives. They receive what should be a complement, "you are pretty", but based on the tone, perception and sometimes the body language of the offending individual, and the addition of "for a black girl" makes it not a complement at all. Comments like this, microaggressions, are said with a frequency that some may not believe. According to Sue, Capodilupo et al. (2007) "racial microaggressions are brief and commonplace daily, verbal, behavioral, and environmental indignities, whether intentional or unintentional, that communicate hostile, derogatory, or negative racial slights and insults to the target person or group" (p. 273). There are three forms of microaggressions; microassault, microinsult, and microinvalidation.

A microassault is "old fashioned racism," there is nothing covert about it; it is very purposeful. In history, examples could be that of the Ku Klux Klan. In this organization, Klansmen, as they called themselves, purposefully discriminated against all people of color. They rallied and organized ensuring that people of color were not afforded the same opportunities as Whites. Another example of microassault would be prior to the civil rights era when public places were designated as "White's Only" and "Colored's Only." At that time one of the most common microassault Black Americans received was being called a "nigger" or a "negro" (Sue, Capodilupo, & Holder, 2008).

Microinsults are when "communications convey rudeness and insensitivity and demean a person's racial heritage or identity" (Sue, Capodilupo et al., 2007, p. 274). This is usually done covertly to minimize a person's background. When a minority is asked, "How did you get that job?" This can be seen as a microinsult as if the minority did not have the job skills necessary to obtain the job on their own. Another example of a microinsult is when a minority is ascribed a level of intelligence that is lower than a White person, simply because of their skin color (Sue, Capodilupo et al., 2007).

Sue, Capodilupo et al., (2007) stated "Microinvalidations are characterized by communications that exclude, negate, or nullify the psychological thoughts, feelings, or experiential reality of a person of color" (p. 274). This type of microaggression seeks to invalidate the experience of a person of color. A minority student usually experiences this when comments are made such as "you are a credit to your race" or telling the person "you are so articulate." This is done to invalidate a person's success in a social situation. Additionally, microinvalidation is usually done to make a minority feel as if their success is only because of their color and someone needed to assist them (Sue, Capodilupo, & Holder, 2008). Additionally microinvalidations is when it is perceived that someone may be too young to have a particular experience or expertise, merely due to the age they are; also known as ageism.

In a qualitative study that focused on two forms of microaggressions (microinsults and microinvalidations), Sue, Capodilupo, and Holder (2008) found that Black Americans felt a sense of powerlessness in relation to Whites. They discussed how the Blacks in this study felt trapped, with little to no control over their situation. Additionally, Sue, Capodilupo, and Holder (2008) stated "the reactions involved cognitive, emotive, and behavioral expressions" (p. 334) when a microaggression was committed against a Black American. Concluding, there was stress present when under this type of aggression, which resulted in a lower performance level on tasks. Sue, Capodilupo, and Holder's study concluded microaggression "creates disparities in education, employment, and health care for the target groups" (p. 330). This type of disparity helps to perpetuate the racial divide between White and Black Americans. It also creates inequities within the student groups. This is when one student feels favored or less valued than another. It makes you reflect and wonder, what would happen if we did more speaking up when situations like this arise?

Unfortunately, microaggressions continue to be a social situation where one group's treats itself as a superior over another. Some of our students experience these microinvalidations, microassault, and microinsults sometimes on a daily basis, which lowers their motivation to attend, participate and be fully engaged in our schools. Some are unaware that it is happening, but they know something is. It is up to us as the adults around them and the educators in front of them to not only stop the injustices taking place, but also be a voice and speak up regarding this issue.

Whiteness as Property

Whiteness is something that has been discussed in research literature about race and African-American life since the early 1990's. Within Critical Race Theory, the notion of "Whiteness as property" is a concept that explains privilege to White's because of the color of their skin. Harris (1995) discussed Whiteness as property in her work when she told the story of her light-skinned grandmother who passed as White in the 1930's and the privileges she was able to have. Those privileges included a job with Whites that catered to middle/upper class White people. Harris examined Whiteness as property in four areas: rights of disposition, rights of use and enjoyment, reputation and status property, and the absolute right to exclude. These four areas have been used by the dominant culture against African Americans and other minorities for a long time.

Rights of disposition are defined as the right to have exclusive rights to property and other alienable rights of a human, which should be inalienable. For example, in the concept of rights of disposition, a White person is able to have a job over a Black person because of the color of their skin. Rights of use and enjoyment of Whiteness is in effect when a White person "used and enjoyed" the privileges only associated with being White. Reputation and status Property of Whiteness is "Whiteness as public reputation and personal property" (Harris, 1995, p. 382). Lastly, the absolute right to exclude makes Whiteness more like a club, a club that is able to exclude others based on the color of their skin. As Harris (1995) described it, "being White was the right to own or hold Whiteness to the exclusion and subordination of Blacks" (p. 383).

Critique of Liberalism

Another tenet of Critical Race Theory is the critique of liberalism. The critique of liberalism has three critical "notions that have been embraced by liberal ideology: the notion of colorblindness, the neutrality of the law, and incremental change" (DeCuir & Dixon, 2004, p. 29). The critique of liberalism has been professed to be one of the slowest processes of Critical Race Theory. It argued that the current educational system is currently a flawed one which does not allow it to be a true "catalyst for social change" because a little at a time is not enough (Ladson-Billings, 1998, p. 12). In the critique of liberalism, Critical Race Theory there to offer a liberating or transformative approach to racial, gender, and class issues. It is designed to navigate social change, via incremental steps within the legal system. Also, in this discourse, "equality, rather than equity is sought" (DeCuir & Dixon, 2004, p. 29). Since equality is sought, the structures that would dismantle racism are not established.

Colorblindness is one example of a liberal concept that Critical Race Theory theorists critique. Liberals believe that if one becomes colorblind and does not acknowledge or see color, he or she will be free from racism (DeCuir & Dixon, 2004). The theory of colorblindness also suggests that everyone can enjoy the same freedoms and the same treatment without regards to race (Gotanda, 1995); which we all know is not true. As Zamudio, Russell, Rios, and Bridgeman (2011) reinforce "race is so much a part of social and cultural heritage it is not only next to impossible to be colorblind–to not take race into account . . ." (p. 23). This expands the idea that the critique of liberalism is also related to interest conversion due to the merging of using legal precedence in order to set the precedence for all people of color. Once again, Critical Race Theorists have found this is a "painstakingly slow process" (Ladson-Billings, 1998, p. 12).

Interest Conversion

Interest conversion is the fourth tenet of Critical Race Theory. Attorney Derrick Bell (1980b) describes it as a principle in which the interest of Blacks only becomes an interest of White elites if the subject is of benefit to White people (p. 523). In interest conversion, it "does not envisage a rational and balanced negotiation between minority groups and White power holders, where change is achieved through the mere force of reason and logic" (Gillborn, 2013, p. 133). In this tenet of Critical Race Theory, Whites or those of the dominant culture are only concerned about issues that arise when it involves their race and is related to their personal progress. When the interests of both Whites and Blacks converge, only then does the issue become a White issue and eventually Blacks are able to progress as a race through this concept.

Interest conversion is related to intersectionality when the interests of Blacks become an interest of Whites; there is usually an intersectional reason. Many researchers cite affirmative action as one of the main examples of interest conversion and intersectionality. It is thought the reason affirmative action was passed because ultimately it was a benefit to White women who came from homes headed by White men. So although affirmative action was designed to assist minorities, because this legislation would assist women, White women were able to benefit from it because of the intersection of gender (Crenshaw, 1989; Delgado & Stefanic, 2001).

Intersectionality

Intersectionality looks at the notion of race, sex, class, gender, sexual orientation, and national origin and how they overlap (Delgado & Stefanic, 2001). Kimberlé Crenshaw (1989) and Angela Harris (1980) developed the notion of intersectionality in order to explain how the antidiscrimination laws during that time failed to address the issues of women of color. The intersections set up the advantages and disadvantages that people of color have when they overlap with another category such as gender.

For example, if you are an African-American female you are met with a deeper level of discrimination according to Crenshaw (1995). This is due to being in more than one of the categories of discriminated people, being female and a person of color. Intersectionality is additionally important in storytelling. In examining a story someone tells, perspective should be considered. When perspective is considered, the group that a discriminated person belongs identifies additional layers of meaning present. Thus, the meanings of the stories told create deeper meanings for the readers (Harris, 1980).

Counter-Storytelling

The fifth tenet of Critical Race Theory is counter-storytelling. Storytelling, counter-storytelling, and narratives are extremely important in Critical Race Theory (Delgado & Stefanic, 2013). They provide a framing for the experiences of people of color. Storytelling serves a purpose. As Delgado (1989) emphasized, it is the process of one naming one's own reality. In naming your own reality, a person is able to experience the sociopolitical structures that plague society; experience how marginalized groups are stereotyped; and how the dominate culture attempts to rationalize the oppression placed on other marginalized groups (Ladson-Billings & Tate, 1995; Solórzano, 1997; Yosso, 2005). A part of naming your own reality, Ladson-Billings (1998) stated, "CRT suggests that current instructional strategies presume that African-American students are deficient" (p. 19). Therefore, if they are already deficient without being assessed for the need of special education in some of society's view, what happens when there is a disability present? This idealization of Critical Race Theory creates the need for stories of those in the African-American and other minority communities to be heard because there is usually the story of the majority or as defined early, the dominant culture, called a master narrative that has been told and perpetrated in the media of what African-American, Hispanic, Asian, and other minority cultures have, what they need, and their experiences instead of individualizing a person's experience. Many times the African-American experience is minimalized because of what the majority thinks and feels about the actions of others (Solórzano & Yosso, 2002).

In Heath's (1983) ethnography, she studied cultural and linguistic patterns in two different working class cities, one White and the other African American. She found the traditions of storytelling ran deep in both cities and although they were different, they were the same. Heath used the linguistic traditions of the communities to teach teachers how to teach students they had not taught and had discarded. Furthermore, the notion of racial differences that would have kept these students and their communities apart actually united them. By learning how to use the language of "schooling," the students were then able to succeed.

Storytelling also has other roles when it comes to outsiders reading a story that is not familiar to theirs. Delgado and Stefanic (2001) established it helps to draw us into what everyday life is like for others. It "invite[s] the reader into a new and unfamiliar world" (p. 41). This invitation helps the reader to feel what the person feels without being there. Counter-storytelling is important because it invites "critical writers . . . to challenge, displace, or mock these pernicious narratives and beliefs" (Delgado & Stefanic, 2001, p. 43). Thus, the stories that are told are used to name discrimination. By naming discrimination, "it can be combated" and society cannot deny it did not happen (Delgado & Stefanic, 2001, p. 44).

Master Narratives

Master narratives are also called "majoritarian stories" in the literature (Ikemoto, 1997; Solórzano & Yosso, 2002; Valencia & Solórzano, 1997). The master narrative is generated from the point of view of racial privilege. It can also be used to distort and silence the experiences of people of color (Ikemoto, 1997). This is due to the stereotypical nature it has. It emphasizes stereotypes of people of color. For example, this stereotypical, narrative makes statements like those that have darker skin and of poverty directly correlates them with bad neighborhoods and bad schools (Valencia & Solórzano, 1997). More specifically, "White teachers, conditioned by their upbringing and the negative stereotypes still reinforced in the media, continue to make negative assumptions about the behavior [and education trajectory] of nonwhite students" (Graybill, 1997, p. 312). Steele and Aronson (1995) argued "whenever African American students perform an explicitly scholastic or intellectual task, they face the threat of confirming or being judged by a negative societal stereotype–a suspicion–about their group's intellectual ability and competence" (p.797), which makes it hard for African Americans to overcome stereotypes.

Other researchers have discussed master or majoritarian narratives and used them in a variety of ways. In critical race theory, the use of a master narrative to represent a group is bound to provide a very narrow depiction of what it means to be Mexican-American,

African-American, White, and so on . . . A master narrative essentializes and wipes out the complexities and richness of a group's cultural life . . . A monovocal account will engender not only stereotyping but also curricular choices that result in representations in which fellow members of a group represented cannot recognize themselves (Montecinos, 1995, pp. 293-294). (Solórzano & Yosso, 2002, p. 27)

This example of the use of the master narrative emphasizes what Valencia and Solórzano (1997) defined as the "biological deficiency model." This model assumes that students of color automatically lack the biological traits to be successful in educational arenas. This master narrative creates inequality before students of color enter schools (Solórzano & Yosso, 2002).

Thus, the counter-narratives that emerge from a CRT lens assist in providing the voices of African Americans an opportunity to speak for themselves and reduce alienation from other members of excluded groups. Counter-storytelling seeks to limit and reduce the effects of master narratives. Again, the master narrative is known as the stereotypical story that is told about a certain race. Likewise, Zamudio et al. (2011) stated, "history is always told from the perspective of the dominant race" (p. 5). Most history lessons in schools are told from a Eurocentric point of view, which is the way society gets its information from; therefore, it is the root of most master narratives. The counter-narratives seek to override the master narrative through a counter-narrative or counter-storytelling. Through the narratives, minorities begin to experience more of the intersectionality of race, class, sex, and gender. Stories are important in education because of the narrative nature of the field, so it is important for those experiencing inequities to tell their stories (Solórzano & Yosso, 2002; Zamudio et al., 2011).

Voices are important because they allow researchers to accurately state the truth of what is happening in the situation, instead of someone telling the story for them (James & Busher, 2006). Delgado and Stefanic (2001) asserted that a person being able to tell their story is powerful and it allows them to no longer suffer in silence and exposes their reality, minimizing the master narrative regarding their situation. When it comes to race, it is important for parents to understand the role race plays in their counter-narrative or their counter-storytelling when discussing their students For so long, master narratives of the dominant culture or thoughts of mere white privilege have dictated how educators interact with minority students. In many situations, the master narrative says, White educators must be the saviors to educate the African-American or minority students who do not have anyone to care for or educate them (Love, 2004).

Reflection

What type of microaggressions do I commit most often with my colleagues? My students? Their families? My superiors?

What steps can I take to be more cognizant of my actions?

Ask yourself, what narratives have I repeated to my own children? To the children in my care? To those around me? How can I reframe the narrative to be more inclusive?

Self-Affirmation

Now that I understand microaggressions, I commit to thinking before speaking and continue to check my internal biases.

STEP 6
~Be Your Own Thermostat~

"The only way to change someone's mind is to connect with them from the heart." ~ Rasheed Ogunlaru ~

On April 16, 1963, towards the end of his civil rights journey, the late Revered Dr. Martin Luther King, Jr.'s Letter from Birmingham Jail, makes a strong claim the people around him are just waiting for justice to happen instead of stepping up and being an advocate. During the Civil Rights era he writes about how the "negro" has gotten used to the phrase "wait." He asserts in this particular letter that since the time of slavery in the United States, systemic oppression has so oppressed enslaved Africans where they were literally beat into submission. Thus training them to be thermometers. They conformed to whatever was happening in their environments for survival sake. Consequently, when they were able to begin making changes, many were still afraid and are currently afraid. It is said by many, systemic oppression of minority groups set the stage for the need of the Civil Rights Era. At the time of this letter, many of the enslaved or descendants of the enslaved had been so oppressed they didn't understand they could be free and do something.

Dr. King and many other leaders admonished minority groups to begin employing the practice of not allowing things to just happen to them without getting up, uniting and doing something about it. Because of the apprehension of many, injustice continued and continues to occur wherever people don't realize they actually embody the power to make changes. Dr. King used this letter not only as a reflection to the work he had done at that time, but as a tool to galvanize others around him to let them know it is not their place to sit and wait for someone else to do it, they need to get up, unite and make a change.

Dr. King's intended audience was eight clergymen, so during this letter, it was appropriate for him to express his feelings about the early Christian church. He discussed how the church used to be one of action, not one that just sits idly by and allow injustice to go uninterrupted. He asserts, "church was not merely a thermometer that recorded the ideas and principles of popular opinion; it was a thermostat that transformed the mores of society." After reading this, one must realize this is definitely not an idea just for churches, but for educational leaders and leaders for social justice and equity. We should all seek to be thermostats. As thermometers we can be moved with the conditions of our environments; as thermostats we control the environment around us and set the tone. In the schools of today we need more thermostats fighting for the health, wellness, and wholeness of our students. But consider this, can you fight for something that you are not? If you are not healthy, well and whole, what will you have to give?

Now you may say, we don't live in the Civil Rights Era any longer; things are better. Well, not exactly. Many of our schools are still segregated by social class and status, attendance boundaries prohibit certain students from attending other schools; parents remain uneducated that they have the right to transfer their students to a school of their choice if their school is underperforming (Title I, Part A, School Choice) we still have educators who are not giving our students equal opportunities and equitable access; we still have educational stakeholders across our states and in our nation who are more about their money and agendas then educating our students by any means necessary. We still have a nation that is divided by race; Klu Klux Klan (KKK) rallies still happening across the United States and racism given a new face; such as the "alt-right" groups. However, as we discussed in earlier steps, change can be difficult, but it can be done.

As educational justice leaders we should always be

on a quest to make the condition of someone else's life better. We should be in the enhancing business, not involved in the tearing down of someone else. But how many times have the conditions of our surroundings frustrated us with things happening around us that we sometimes just quit? We quit fighting for what we believe because of being discouraged? Why? Usually because we hit some form of opposition. Have you considered opposition is what makes one stronger? In the words of German philosopher, Friedrich Nietzsche (1887) "that which does not kill us, makes us stronger." As we continue to make steps to change the master narrative that states that one culture is more superior to others, we will develop the grit and the mental toughness to ultimately change culture. In thinking about this concept, what are you doing to ensure you are emotionally healthy enough to be a thermostat?

Emotional Health

Daniel Goleman, author of Emotional Intelligence (1995) is one of the modern thought leaders who reflect on the work of Salovey and Mayer (1990) who first used the concept of emotional intelligence. Emotional intelligence has been defined as one being more aware of our emotions and what the positive results could be. Goleman (1995) states that by doing this, not only are we able to have more control over our emotions, but we are able to empathize with other people that we come in contact with because we become better listeners. Think about it, when was the last time you truly listened to someone without thinking about what you are going to say next? When you become a better listener, the condition of your emotional health goes up.

Another concept in emotional health directly connects to the school system. Cohen (2006) writes how the skills and dispositions needed for one to participate in a democracy connect with the skills needed in a school system. I assert these are the skills needed for one to be their own thermostat. The notion of "being able to listen to ourselves and others, the ability to be critical and reflective, the ability to be flexible problem-solvers and decision maker, including the ability to resolve conflict in creative, non violent ways, to communicate abilities and have collaborative capacities is what is needed to create change in a school setting (p. 204). This notion sets the stage for social emotional learning that must take place in the educator first before you are able to teach it to children. You cannot claim to be a collaborator but are unable to be a flexible problem solver and decision maker.

Many schools across the nation have moved to developing social emotional learning standards and character education. It is thought that many of the soft skills taught by schools in decade's prior are the skills that students lack that prohibit them from being innovative, collaborators and critical thinkers. Thus making it important for the educator to understand their emotional health to move students from merely being a thermometer to a thermostat.

To examine your own personal emotional health, are you practicing self-care? When you have a bad day, what do you do with that day? Do you continue to speak negative OR do you speak positive affirming words? Contemplate, in your environment of influence, have you been the thermostat or the thermometer? Remember, the thermometer reacts to the environment by changing with the temperature of the people in the room. The thermostat regulates the environment. It determines if it is hot or cold. So which one are you? You wrote your non-negotiables in step two, have you considered those in your response of what makes you a thermometer or a thermostat?

Reflection

What is my response to my non-negotiables? Does it make me a thermometer or a thermostat? What is my response to others non-negotiables?

STEP 7
~Asset Based Thinking~

"If you change the way you look at things, the things you look at change." ~ Dr. Wayne Dyer

Now that you realize you were created to be a thermostat, you have to go back to the way you see the world and the students you serve. Having an asset-based mindset is important because it sets the stage for your actions. Regrettably, many educators operate from a deficit mindset that is usually created by a racial stereotype. This type of judgment is based on a master narrative. Master narratives are also called "majoritarian stories" in the literature (Ikemoto, 1997; Solórzano & Yosso, 2002; Valencia & Solórzano, 1997). The master narrative is generated from the point of view we recognized in an earlier step when we discussed privilege. Racial stereotypes in schools are usually used to distort and silence the experiences of people of color. For example, this stereotypical narrative makes statements like those that have darker skin and of poverty directly correlates them with bad neighborhoods and bad schools (Ikemoto, 1997; Valencia & Solórzano, 1997). More specifically, "White teachers, conditioned by their upbringing and the negative stereotypes still reinforced in the media, continue to make negative assumptions about the behavior [and education trajectory] of nonwhite students" (Graybill, 1997, p. 312). Steele and Aronson (1995) argued "whenever African American students perform an explicitly scholastic or intellectual task, they face the threat of confirming or being judged by a negative societal stereotype–a suspicion–about their group's intellectual ability and competence" (p.797), which makes it hard for African Americans and many minority groups to overcome stereotypes.

Other researchers have discussed master or majoritarian narratives and used them in a variety of ways. In critical race theory,

> the use of a master narrative to represent a group is bound to provide a very narrow depiction of what it means to be Mexican-American, African-American, White, and so on . . . A master narrative essentializes and wipes out the complexities and richness of a group's cultural life . . . A monovocal account will engender not only stereotyping but also curricular choices that result in representations in which fellow members of a group represented cannot recognize themselves (Montecinos, 1995, pp. 293-294). (Solórzano & Yosso, 2002, p. 27)

This example of the use of the master narrative emphasizes what Valencia and Solórzano (1997) defined as the "biological deficiency model." This model assumes that students of color automatically lack the biological traits to be successful in educational arenas. This master narrative creates inequality before students of color enter schools (Solórzano & Yosso, 2002).

Thus, the counter-narratives that emerge from a CRT lens assist in providing the voices of African Americans an opportunity to speak for themselves and reduce alienation from other members of excluded groups. Counter-storytelling seeks to limit and reduce the effects of master narratives. Again, the master narrative is known as the stereotypical story that is told about a certain race.

However, once the racial stereotypical threat is realized by a student, they become anxious about his or her inadequacy as a learner because they believe their personal failure on an assignment or test will confirm the negative stereotype associated with his or her race, socioeconomic status, gender, or language background. This type of anxiety can also be a form of internalized oppression whereby the student internalizes the negative social messages about his racial group, begins to believe them, and loses confidence (Hammond, 2015, p. 91)

    The starting point for holding all students to the same high standards is the deconstruction and rejection of what is known as deficit thinking and the reconstruction of positive images of able and engaged students. Deficit thinking is another way of saying that we blame the students or their families for their lack of school success because we see them as being in some way deficient. In other words, we equate difference with deficiency and place the onus on them to change. Although educators may not use this transformative leadership language of deconstructing and reconstructing knowledge frameworks, many scholars argue for the necessity of rejecting deficit thinking and holding high expectations for all students. Almost 20 years ago, Wagstaff and Fusarelli (1995) conducted a study in which they found that the single most important factor in the academic achievement of minority students is the principal's explicit rejection of deficit thinking (p. 38). By rejecting deficit thinking, the principal was able to ensure students received a fair opportunity to succeed. Considering if the principal had this effect on students, what difference would it make for classrooms teachers to take this same approach?

    In reviewing what could be the result if educators continue in deficit based thinking, one must also consider the occurrences of school violence and the impact of school safety. The strategies of both prevention and intervention to counteract all of the things happening in schools and the surroundings communities to predict further violence, is important. Regarding intervention, Denenberg et al. (1998) discover when authoritative figures follow up on possible threats or dangerous events, they will do a great service to the students they serve. In their research, they indicate most school districts are unprepared to deal with the issues that plague children who are "at risk for violence" (p. 33). They do not have anyone in place to teach them how to use conflict resolution and problem solving skills. As a result, the authors discovered, the propensity for violence, both in school and in later life, can best be cured in the long run by enlarging students' understanding and self-confidence. Until that goal is achieved, however, it is prudent for school districts to rely for their safety on well-drilled, consensus-based violence prevention and response teams (p. 35).

Fox & Savage (2009) recommend that by projecting a "student centered" approach, making changes to the services offered to students that include counseling despite insurance, should improve the stress and well-being of all students on campus. Whereas, keeping all students safe despite resources should be on the forefront of our minds.

In considering at which stage it is important to look at how violence affects children, Guerra, Huesmann and Spindler (2003) investigated how when elementary school children are exposed to violence at an early age, it leads to an "increase in aggression, normative beliefs about aggression and aggressive fantasy" (p. 1561). In their 6-year study, they studied a large number of students between 1st and 6th grades in 21 schools in Chicago. Data was collected between 1 and 6 times for each student in the study in the urban and inner-city communities. They monitored the student's levels of aggression from the peers and teachers point of view. Guerra, et al. (2009) found students were more aggressive during their early elementary years and the way to prevent it was to "minimize children's exposure to violence and to increase their safety" (p. 1574). Bosworth, Ford, and Hernandez (2011) agree students have the need to feel safe and staff needs to be equipped to handle their perceptions of safety. Guerra et al. (2009) and Bosworth, et al. (2011), suggest parents, schools and communities do this by creating opportunities for students to practice being nonaggressive and learn how to deal with conflict appropriately which takes an asset based mentality on the part of the educator. Therefore it is important that even at an early age, children should not be exposed to violence because it can affect them.

It was recommended schools have social workers working to assist school staff and parents connect. Schools should be encouraged to identify areas on campus that were prone to violence and create teams of stakeholders to find out why. Many studies have found the most successful school safety programs were those who considered the needs of the city, school, and community.

Unsafe schools have been categorized as those with "decreased school attendance, grades, and participation in school activities, and increased negative attitudes toward schools, school avoidance, fear, posttraumatic stress, and misbehavior" (Hong & Eatmon, 2012, p. 428). Therefore another way of creating safe schools is to change the perception of the school community from within the family, school and neighborhood structure. Thus, the framework for asset based thinking. Continuing to come together, highlighting the positives in an individual, their culture, the results would be amazing for our students.

However, there has been a long-standing reluctance on the part of American society in general and the educational establishment in particular to recognize and remedy the existence and ill effects of privileges in certain groups or part of society. The privileged groups that currently exist in our nation are the one to be responsible for the misfortune of the different minority groups when it relates to education and safety.

Educator Nancy Fraser speaks to the issue of privileged groups and discusses methods to remedy this problem. The discussion addresses two diverse viewpoints of how to approach the issue of redistribution and recognition from within the concepts of equity. Fraser refers to this as the redistribution-recognition dilemma (p. 92). The politics of recognition highlights group differences and recognizes the injustices offered upon certain groups within a society. (Heidegren, 2004). In contrast, redistribution politics attempts to de-emphasize group differences and downplays those same injustices. Dumas (2009) takes the position that the politics of recognition emphasizes how particular groups are "subject to marginalization, discrimination, intimidation, even death on the basis of how the society has constructed that group's social legitimacy" (p. 82). Fraser then draws a contrast between two types of remedies, transformative and affirmative. Transformative remedies attempt to address and rectify root causes of social inequities. Affirmative remedies looks at social inequities without looking at where they are coming from and trying to change the root of the problem. With this conceptualization, one must realize that we must be transformative in our approach to students. Constantly and consistently searching for the root of the problems that ail our progress.

Dumas (2009) solution is the idea of recognition as a process that restores different structures of lack of respect and the affect it has on self-esteem. It is described the politics of recognition as a concept that marginalizes a specific group and discriminates them due to their social economic status.

The students in our current system need to be able to receive equitable services as other schools in our nation and be recognized for their achievements and the culture in which they live. We should all carry the belief that students should be provided with equitable education, school safety, resources, and instruction from an asset based model. As we discussed, some students do not feel safe attending schools in their communities and we must be willing to take on the role of making them feel like their culture, background and upbringing allows them to come to the table each day with something to offer (Bosworth, et al., 2011; Hong & Eamon, 2012; Astor, et al., 2005; Guerra, et al., 2003).

Reflection

What can I do in my daily practice to ensure I am looking at the positives of a student, instead of the negatives? How do I engage in asset-based thinking more than I engage in deficit-based thinking?

STEP 8
~Watch Your Conversations~

"Every child needs a champion" ~ Rita F. Pierson

Parents look at their roles in very different ways when their children go to school. Teachers, administrators, community members and other stakeholders often view the same child in a different way. Additionally if the child has a disability or exceptionality, it sometimes means parents must take on additional roles to ensure their students receive what they need in a school setting. Consider, when a child enter school for the first time in preschool or in Kindergarten, parents usually assume the role of the protector because for the first time in many cases, their children are out of their primary care for most of their waking day. Occasionally with the role of the protector, many parents are immediately on the defense as it relates to their children if anything happens out of the ordinary.

As Clark (1963) asserted, "no normal parent would deliberately block his child's opportunity to obtain preparation he needs in order to meet the present and the future" (p. 9). Thus, it is important for educators to understand the notion that parents do what they think needs to be done in order to assist their children in meeting their full potential. Many times, the perceived attitudes of a parent may turn the educator off or be offensive, but it is important to note it is not personal, but it is the champion role of the parent that emerges.

Barton, Drake, Perez, St. Louis, and George (2004) conducted a study on parental roles in urban education. Urban in this context is the setting of a predominately minority community. They defined parental roles as something a parent does in a school setting; also seen as more of an "object or an outcome" (Barton et al., p. 6). It is also defined as "a set of relationships and actions that cut across individuals, circumstances, and events that are produced and bounded by the context in which engagement takes place" (Barton et al., p. 11). This relates to many area school districts in Southern California, as there are many that are predominately Hispanic and African American.

When thinking about familial support, Mackintosh, Myers and Goin-Kochel (2005) discussed how economic status could often dictate how parents receive information and support from schools. Furthermore, in their study they found "the top 5% [of families] used 12 or more sources of support, while the bottom 5% reported having no supports whatsoever" (p. 50). This research denotes that some parents respond negatively to the school setting because they have no other choice, but to work, leaving the schooling of their children to the educators. However, when parents do not respond, it occasionally results in the educator thinking that parents do not care because of their lack of attention; when really it is due to economics.

Mandell, Listerud et al. (2002) asserted that African-American parents are less likely to reach out for support than other races. With this startling research, we must change the master narrative about the notion that minority parents don't care and do our job as educators to see what we can do to eliminate and decrease the barriers. Parental engagement is important, but you can only do that if you watch your conversations. When engaging parents, educators must have a certain level of sensitivity and connectivity that relates to the families one serves.

In school settings, teachers and parents see their roles in very different ways (Huang & Mason, 2008). Traditionally, the teachers have a "sense of formality and a focus on intellectual development, parents may view their children in more holistic and personal ways" (Hong, 2011, p. 13). Therefore, some educators struggle with helping schools and homes find the connection. Also, research shows that African-American parents are more alienated from the school setting than their White counterparts (Huang & Mason, 2008; Stoner & Angell, 2006). Without that connection, there will continue to be a struggle for "legitimacy, power, and appreciation creates tangible distrust between teachers and parents and between families and schools leading each party to approach the other defensively" (Hong, 2011, p. 14). Clark (1963) established that parents from minority groups, especially African Americans, have a greater responsibility in raising their children than non-minorities. They must take on the additional role of being sensitive to the feelings of their child in social situations. In doing so, this will help them build their self-esteem resulting in higher achievement in school. Without being sensitive to their children, they could be seen as breaking the spirit of their children because they fail to validate the child's experience. Thus, as the educator partnering with the parent, the conversation will have a positive tone, resulting in positive outcomes for their children.

Understandably, parental roles are seen as a top need in schools to mend the struggle of power. It is known to researchers that relationships, influence, and parent education are a key part in making sure parents are able to take on the influential roles needed for their children to succeed academically (Huang & Mason, 2008). In schools, it is an ongoing struggle for both groups to collaborate consistently and effectively. Unfortunately, there are times where there is the perceived family structure instead of viewing the family as an individual. This incorrect perception perpetuates a stereotype that pushes parents out of our schools. It lowers the engagement and ultimately hurts the students we desire to witness succeed.

Overcoming perception is the notion that requires parents to confront the issues in education for their children in order to obtain the proper education, services, accommodations, and modifications for their children. As Barton et al. (2004) asserted, when parents that take on multiple roles in their students' education, their children obtain a better education because the level of engagement is up.

The job of parenting varies at different stages of a child's life. Franklin and Franklin (1985) described the inherent role of a parent to be a "nurturer and a teacher" (p. 175). Parenting can also be defined as "the process of taking care of children until they are able to care for themselves" (Merriam-Webster Dictionary, n.d.). Thus it is important for parents to play an active role in ensuring they are available to their children to meet their needs and the educator must be open to having crucial, courageous and taking a non-stereotypical stance when thinking about the perceived family structure.

Many families would love to partner with schools and communities for the betterment of their students well being. So as educators we must do our part in ensuring we are readily available to partner with parents. Through this partnership, the assumptions that parents don't care, parents just like to scream at the educators, parents always defend their children, parents don't want to know the truth about their students will be a misnomer because the partnership for improved communication will result is achieving this step of cultural proficiency.

Reflection

Am I ready to have some crucial, courageous and understanding conversations with the families I serve?
If not, I am determined to make ____ steps. If I am, I will continue to do _____

Step 9
~Can you relate?~

"All of the great leaders have had one characteristic in common: it was the willingness to confront unequivocally the major anxiety of their people in their time. This, and not much else, is the essence of leadership."
~ John Kenneth Galbraith

Being relatable is a desired quality of all educators. To be effective in the 21st Century, you must be able to relate to the needs of the world around you. Being responsive to a student's culture can disrupt the comfort of what we are used to in our classrooms in our schools. It is the responsive ability to confront the discomfort of being on the learning end instead of the teaching end. In this step towards cultural proficiency, one must be open to allowing the student to be the teacher. Allowing them to express their thoughts, feelings, actions and aspects of even deep culture without feeling the condemnation from the educator. Empowering the students to utilize their slang and their current technologies not only raise the relevance of the educator, but it solidifies the relatable qualities of the educator.

One thing to caution is the slang our students use to communicate with one another changes so rapidly that it takes an educator to be in constant relationship with their students to keep up. The tone, sentence structure and responses to our questions are usually dependent on the depth of the relationship the students have with their educator. If the educator has a strong but non-judgmental, non-shock factor response to the things the students say, students are usually more apt to keep the educator updated with the most recent information.

In considering technology, it is often discussed how our students are digital natives. Computers, tablets and smart phones are placed in student's hands before they can even speak. Many homes and even cities have Wi-Fi connections and students do not even know what dial up Internet was. Consequently, Wi-Fi is a staple of their culture. They have no idea that when the Internet first emerged, wireless did not exist. For example, students do not realize that when the Internet was used our home phone lines could not be used at the same time. They have no idea that we used to have 5x7 size floppy disks that would carry information and if they had any speck of dust on them that they would not work. They have no idea families were considered "rich" if they had car phones that were plugged into the car and computers that were the size of wall unit televisions.

With this thinking our students and educators alike are presented with the notion that we are from two different cultures as it relates to slang and technology. Technology is moving so rapidly that information is literally at the fingertips of anyone who needs it. We now store things in the "cloud" and as long as you have Internet connection, you have access to most of your documents that you have stored there. You have access to countless amounts of sources. That is culture.

Back when I first began my schooling, I would have to go to the library for hours to do research. I would have to use the card catalogue, pull the card and then hope that when I went to the shelf to pick up the book, that it was actually there. However, we know that was not always the case because the book may not be there. I could spend hours just searching for books to do research. Now when you go to the library, you look on a computer and it can tell you if it is there or not and when it is proposed to return. Also, most libraries have an Internet database and if you don't want to, you do not have to leave home to do any research. You can do it from your home. This is culture!!

Technology has brought us to a place where access and information gathering is happening at such a rapid pace, we must make strides to ensure we keep up. We must think about equity in technology and remember that although almost everyone has access to a smartphone, not all of our students have access to consistent Wi-Fi. Conducting a survey in your classroom is ideal to see what your students have access to and what their needs are. As educators for educational justice, we must be committed to ensure the emotional health of our students is intact and sometimes the lack of knowledge regarding technology and slang diminishes our relateability. This means as an educator, we remain relatable when we are able to empathize with our students and where they are. We should also be in the practice of following up with them to ensure they are thriving in their environments.

Reflection:

Do you have conversations with students as you are walking the halls of your school? Are you consistently seeking out a few to build stronger intentional relationships to create a bridge for you to know the slang? What methods do you use daily to stay connected to the students and families you serve? How do you identify the cultural differences in slang and technology in order to stay relevant?

Step 10
~Be the Change~

"Be the change you want to see in the world." ~ Mahatma Gandhi

Being the change is more about changing yourself then changing the world. You cannot bring change to the environment if you are not willing to take an introspective look and respond to your internal biases. By completing all nine steps so far, you have shown your commitment to desiring to be more culturally proficient. Being the change is an ongoing process. It is an ongoing process of knowing who you are, staying in line with your purpose, reaching towards the students you have signed up to serve and connecting them with their purpose.

Being the change takes the 4 C's; courage, conviction, consistency, and commitment. We must be courageous. We must ensure that we are not conforming to status quo just to get by, get a promotion or to be seen. We must be courageous enough to challenge the world around us to be equitable by providing students with what they need, when they need it. We must be willing to be courageous enough to challenge master narratives and stereotypes about the students and families we serve, to bring about positive change in our immediate environments. We must not allow others to try to shrink our passion or our commitment to our students because of the moves other are failing to make for our students. We must re-write narratives.

We must have conviction to speak up when our colleagues make that racially or sexually charged statement. We must have the conviction to not allow injustice and inequities to continue in front of our eyes. We must be better than that. We must carry the conviction that we can be the thermostats in our sphere of influence and change what we see. We must be bold in our conviction, not allowing anyone or anything to change our growth mindset.

We must be consistent in our approach to the students, families, communities, and other stakeholders that are being served. Yes, it is a constant endeavor to stay culturally proficient. We cannot go through all the 10 steps and not have to repeat a step here and there due to the situation or circumstance. Things happen, society changes, new challenges arise daily and we must be the consistent educator that strives for excellence at all times.

Ultimately, we must be committed to the process of change. By committing to ourselves, our community and our world will change not only you but those who you have come in contact with. In order to continue this quest for culturally proficiency you must stay connected. Read the newspaper at least weekly, if not daily. Find and subscribe to the weekly and sometimes daily news briefs produced by many of the trusted educational professionals. By staying current with organizations like EdTrust, EdCal, EdSource, Teaching Tolerance, you will be on the right track to remain culturally proficient!

Reflection:

What are some immediate changes you can make after finishing this book? What are some changes that are down the road?

References

Anderson, S.A. (1997). Understanding teacher change: Revisiting the Concerns Based Adoption Model. Curriculum Inquiry, 27:3, 331-337.

Banks, J. (2006). Race, culture, and education: The selected works of James Banks. New York: Routledge.

Benabou, R. (1996). Equity and efficiency in human capital investment: The local connection. Review of Economic Studies. 63, 237-264.

Berlant, L. & Freeman, E. (1992). Queer Nationality. New Americanists 2: National Idenities and Post Narratives, 19(1), 149-180.

Berliner, D. (2006). Our impoverished view of educational reform. The Teachers College Record. 108:6, 949-995.

Blackmore, J. (2002). Leadership for socially just schooling: More substance and less style in high risk, low-trust times? Journal of School Leadership, 12(2), 198-222.

Blasé, J. & Bjork, L.G. (2010). The micropolitics of educational change and reform: Cracking open the black box. In Hargreaves, A., Lieberman, A., Fullan, M., & Hopkins, D. (Eds.) Second International Handbook of Educational Change (pp. 237-258). New York: Springer.

Bouie, E. (2012). The impact of bureaucratic structure, scientific management, and institutionalism on standards-based educational reform. Mercer Journal of Educational Leadership, 1:1, 1-21.

Bourdieu, P. (1980). Le capital social: Notes provisoires. Actes de la Recherche in sciences sociales. 31:2-3.

Bourdieu, P. (1989). Social space and symbolic power. Sociological Theory. 7:1, 14-25.

Brewer, D.J., Hentschke, G.C., & Eide, E.R. (2010). Theoretical concepts in the economics of education. In Brewer, D.J. & McEwan P.J. (Eds.) Economics in education (pp. 3 – 7). Amsterdam: Academic Press.

Bull, B. (2004) A political theory of social justice in American schools. In Rodriguez, G. & Rolle, R.A., (Eds.) To what ends and by what means (pp. 9-34). New York: Routledge.

Chia, P. (2008). The sun never sets on 'Marx'? (Marx) Colonizing Postcolonial theory (Said/ Spivak/ Bhabha). Journal for the study of the New Testament, 30(4), 481-488.

Ciulla, J.B. ed. (2004). Ethics, the heart of leadership. Westport, CT: Praeger Publishers.

Cohen, J. (2006). Social, emotional, ethical, and academic education: Creating a climate for learning, participation in democracy, and well-being. Harvard educational Review, 76(2), 201-237.

Coleman, J. (1988). Social capital and the creation of human capital. The American Journal of Sociology. 94: S95-S120.

Collins, J. (2001). Good to great. New York: HarperCollins.

Delgado, R. & Stefanic, J. (2001). Critical Race Theory: An introduction. New York: New York University Press.

Drake & Goldring (2014) Politics in school engagement and decisions in Lindle, J. (Ed.). (2014). Political Contexts of Educational Leadership: ISLLC Standard Six. Routledge.

Dumas, M. (2007). Redistribution and Recognition in Urban Education Research. In J. Anyon Theory and educational research: Toward critical social explanation (pp.81-107). New York, NY: Routledge.

Dumas, M. (2009). Theorizing redistribution and recognition in urban education research. In J. Anyon (Ed.), Theory and educational research: Toward critical social explanation. New York: Routledge, 81-107.

Eden, D. (1984). Self-fulfilling prophecy as a management tool: Harnessing Pygmalion. Academy of management Review, 9(1), 64-73.

Foster, W. (1986). Paradigms and promises: New approaches to educational administration. Buffalo, NY: Prometheus Books.

Freire, P. (1970). The pedagogy of the oppressed. New York: Seabury.

Galor, O. & Tsiddon, D. (1997). The distribution of human capital and economic growth. Journal of Economic Growth. 2:1, 93-124.

Goldfarb, K.P. & Grinberg, J. (2002). Leadership for social justice: Authentic participation in the case of community center in Caracas, Venezula. Journal of School Leadership, 12, 157-173.

Goleman, D. (2006). Emotional intelligence. Bantam.

Heckman, J. (2000). Policies to foster human capital. Research in Economics. 54, 3-56.

Heckman, J. (2006). Skill formation and the economics of investing in disadvantaged children. Science. 312: 1900-1902.

Heckman, J. & Masterov, D. (2004). The productivity argument for investing in young children. (Working Paper 5, Invest in Kids Working Group Committee for Economic Development). Retrieved from NICHD htto://jenni.uchicago.edu/Invest/.

Heidegren, C.G. (2004). Book review: Recognition

and social theory. Acta Sociologica. 47(4), 365-373.

Heubert, J.P. (Ed.). (1999). Law and school reform: Six strategies for promoting educational equity. Yale University Press.

Horkheimer, M. & Adorno, T.W. (1972). Dialectic of Enlightenment, New York: Seabury.

Howard, T. (2010). Why race and culture matter in school: Closing the achievement gap in America's classrooms. New York, NY: Teachers College Press.

Ikemoto, G.S. & Marsh, J.A. (2007). Cutting through the "data-driven" mantra: Different conceptions of data-driven decision making. National Society for the Study of Education Yearbook, 106(1), 105-131.

Ishimaru, A. (2012). From heroes to organizers: Principals and education organizing in urban school reform. Educational Administration Quarterly, 49(3), 3-51.

James, E.H. (2000). Race-related differences in promotions and support: Underlying effects of human and social capital. Organization Science. 11:5, 493-508.

Kantor, H. (1991). Education, social reform, and the state: ESEA and federal education policy in the 1960s. American Journal of Education, 100(1), 47-83.

Kimmel, Michael S. (2009). Privilege: A Reader. Westview Press. pp. 1, 5, 13–26.

Klebanov, P. & Brooks-Gunn, J. (2006). Cumulative, human capital, and psychological risk in the context of early intervention. Annuals New York Academy of Sciences. 1094: 63-82.

Kumashiro, K. (2000). Toward a theory of anti-oppressive education. Review of Educational Research 70(1), 25-53.

Ladson-Billings, G. (1992). Reading between the

lines and beyond the pages: A culturally relevant approach to literacy teaching. Theory into Practice, 31(4), 312-330.

Ladson-Billings, G. (1998). Just what is critical race theory and what's it doing in a nice field like education? Qualitative Studies in Education, 11(1), 7-24.

Ladson-Billings, G. & Tate, W.F. (1995). Toward a critical race theory of education. Teachers College Record, 97(1), 47-68.

Lijenstrom, H. & Svedin, U. (Eds.) (2005). Micro, meso, macro: Addressing complex systems couplings. Hackensack, N.J.: World Scientific Publishing.

Lindsey, R. B., Robins, K. N., & Terrell, R. D. (2003). *Cultural proficiency: A manual for school leaders*. Corwin Press.

Marshall, C. & Gerstl-Pepin, C. (2005). Micropolitics. Re-Framing educational politics for social justice (pp. 101-126). Boston: Allyn and Bacon.

Mayer, J. D., & Geher, G. (1996). Emotional intelligence and the identification of emotion. Intelligence, 22(2), 89-113.

McKenzie, K.B., Christman, D.E., Hernandez, F., Fierro, E., Capper, C.A., Dantley, M., Gonzalez, M.L., Cambron-McCabe, N., & Scheurich, J.J. (2008). From the field: A proposal for social justice. Educational Administration Quarterly, 44(1), 111-138.

McLoyd, V. (1998). Socioeconomic disadvantage and child development. American Psychologist. 53:2, 185-204.

Minow, M., Shweder, R.A. & Markus, H.R. (2008). Just schools: Pursuing equality in societies of difference. New York: Russell Sage Foundation.

Mirci, P. (2007). "Kurt Lewin's Model of Changing

an Institution: How Might the Change Process be described." Changing the way adults view learning for themselves and students: A resource for the professional development of teachers and administrators [Step 4].

Moll, L., Amanti, C., Neff, D., Gonzalez, N. (1992). Funds of knowledge for teaching: Using a qualitative approach to connect homes and classrooms. Theory into Practice, 31(2), 132-141.

Nietzsche, F. (2010). *On the genealogy of morals and ecce homo*. Vintage.

O'Connor, C., Hill, L.D., Robinson, S.R. Who's at risk in school and what's race got to do with it? Review of Research in Education, 33(1), 1-34.

Portes, A. (1998). Social capital: Its origins and applications in modern sociology. Annual Sociology, 24:1-24.

Portes, A. (2000). The two meanings of social capital. Sociological Forum. 15:1, 1-12.

Rich, A. (1996). Compulsory heterosexuality and lesbian existence in feminism and sexuality. Jackson & Scott.

Riehl, C. (2000). The principal's role in creating inclusive schools for diverse students: A review of normative, empirical, and critical literature on the practice of educational administration. Review of Educational Research. 70(1), 55-81.

Sandel, M. (2009). Justice: What's the right thing to do? New York, NY: Farrar, Straus, and Giroux.

Sergiovanni, T. J. (2007). Leadership as stewardship: Who's serving who? In Fullan, M. (Ed.), The Jossey-Bass Reader on Educational Leadership, 2nd Edition (pp. 75-92). San Francisco: John Wiley & Sons.

Shannon, P. (Ed.) (2001). Becoming political:

Readings and writing in the politics of literacy education. Portsmouth, NH: Heiremann.

Shapiro, J.P. & Stefkovich, J.A. (2001). Ethical leadership and decision making in education: Applying theoretical perspectives to complex dilemmas. Mahwah, NJ: Lawrence Erlbaum.

Shaprio, J. & Stefkovich, J. (2005). Ethical leadership and decision making in education. [2nd Edition]. Mahwah, New Jersey: Lawrence Erlbauh Associates.

Skiba, R., Simmons, A., Ritter, S., Kohler, K., Henderson, M., Wu, T. (2006). The context of minority disproportionality: Practitioner perspectives on special education referral. Teacher College Record, 108(7), 1424-1459.

Skrla, L., McKenzie, K., & Scheurich, J.J. (2009). Using equity audits to create equitable and excellent schools. Thousand Oaks, CA: Corwin

Skrla, L., Scheurich, J.J., Garcia, J., Nolly, G. (2010) Equity audits: A practical leadership tool for developing equitable and excellent schools. In C. Marshall & M. Oliva. Leadership for social justice: Making revolutions in education (pp. 259- 283). Boston: Allyn & Bacon.

Skrla, L., Scheurich, J.J., Garcia, J., Nolly, G. (2010) Equity audits: A practical leadership tool for developing equitable and excellent schools. In C. Marshall & M. Oliva. Leadership for social justice: Making revolutions in education (pp. 259- 283). Boston: Allyn & Bacon.

Smith, C. S., & Hung, L. C. (2008). Stereotype threat: Effects on education. Social Psychology of Education, 11(3), 243-257.

Starratt, R.J. (1994). Building an ethical school: A practical response to the moral crisis in schools. Washington, D.C.: Falmer Press.

Sue, D.W., Capodilupo, C.M., Holder, A.M.B. (2008). Racial microaggressions in the life experience of Black Americans. Professional Psychology: Research and Practice, 39(3), 329-336.

Sue, D.W., Capodilupo, C.M., Torino, G.C., Bucceri, J.M., Holder, A.M.B., Nadal, K.L., & Esquilin, M. (2007). Racial microaggressions in everyday life: Implications for clinical practice. American Psychologist Association, 62(4), 271-286.

Sue, D.W., Lin, A.I., Torino, G.C., Capodilupo, C.M., Rivera, D.P. (2009). Racial microaggressions and difficult dialogues on race in the classroom. Cultural Diversity and Ethnic Minority Psychology, 15(2), 183-190.

Sue, D.W., Nadal, K.L., Capodilupo, C.M., Lin, A.I, Torino, G.C., Rivera, D.P. (2008). Racial microaggressions against Black Americans: Implications for counseling. Journal of Counseling and Development, 86(3), 330-338.

Theoharis, G. (2007). Social justice educational leaders and resistance: Toward a theory of social justice leadership. Educational Administration Quarterly, 43(2), 221-258.

Vaught, S. E., Castagno, A.E. (2008). "I don't think I'm a racist": Critical race theory, teacher attitudes, and structural racism. Race and Ethnicity and Education, 11(2), 95-113.

Wayne, S., Liden, R., Kraimer, M., & Graf, I. (1999). The role of human capital, motivation, and supervisor sponsorship in predicting career success. Journal of Organizational Behavior. 20, 577-595.

West, C. (2004). Democracy matters. New York: Penguin Books.

Wilkinson III, J.H. (1978). The Supreme Court and southern school desegregation, 1955-1970: A history and analysis. Virginia Law Review, 64(4), 485-559.

Young, I.M. (1990). Five faces of oppression. Justice and the politics of difference. Princeton, NJ: Princeton University Press.

For more information or to schedule a workshop with
Dr. Casaundra Monique McNair,
please visit
www.casaundramcnair.com

www.ingramcontent.com/pod-product-compliance
Lightning Source LLC
Chambersburg PA
CBHW070547300426
44113CB00011B/1817